SOUND
SIGHT-READING

for CONCERT BAND

Music-Reading and Performance Concepts

Brian **BECK** | Scott **WATSON** | Robert **SHELDON**

Alfred Music
P.O. Box 10003
Van Nuys, CA 91410-0003
alfred.com

ISBN-10: 1-4706-4290-5
ISBN-13: 978-1-4706-4290-7

Instrument photos courtesy of Yamaha Corporation of America Band & Orchestral Division

Welcome to *Sound Sight-Reading!*

You have been learning a truly special skill in band: decoding notes, rhythms, and more as you encounter them in written music, then performing them on your instrument. *You've been learning to read music!* The purpose of *Sound Sight-Reading* is to provide you with strategies for doing this accurately, efficiently, and independently so you can play better, both alone and in ensemble music.

What Is Sight-Reading?

Sight-reading is the ability to read and perform music at sight, without the benefit of prior practice or of another person (such as your band director) demonstrating it for you. *Sound Sight-Reading* provides valuable strategies for learning to do this well, including:

Aim for the S.T.A.R.S.!

The letters of the acronym, S.T.A.R.S., stand for important musical elements you should observe prior to performing any music*:

1. **Signatures (time and key)**—How many beats per measure? What kind of note receives one beat? What notes in this line are affected by the key signature?

2. **Tempo (and other expressive markings)**—How fast and with what character should the music be played?

3. **Accidentals**—Where do they occur and for how long before returning to the "normal" (diatonic) note(s)?

4. **Rhythms**—Are there any complex rhythms I need to figure out? How will I count rhythmic subdivisions?

5. **Signs (repeats, endings, segno, coda, etc.)**—What is the "roadmap" for this piece?

Note the five S.T.A.R.S. elements in the example below:

* Note: Not all music includes each of these five items.

Break It Down (Progressive Success)

When first encountering any music, especially if it seems challenging, try focusing on one or more separate musical elements before performing the whole. Achieve success in steps!

Any/all of the following five steps may be employed to "break down" the passage above:

1. **SPEAK**—Say the note names aloud in the order they occur in the music.

2. **COUNT/CLAP**—Say the counts for the music. Use the counting system presented in this book, or one shared with you by your instructor. We recommend speaking normally the counts for the notes but whispering the counts for the rests. When rhythmically confident, clap rhythms (counting aloud or internally), clasping hands to show longer, held durations.

3. **SING**—Sing or "chant" the note names while following the general contour of the music. We use note names throughout the book, but scale degree numbers or solfege syllables may be used as well.

4. **ARTICULATE/FINGER**—Execute with the tongue the onset of notes in the passage, either blowing air (with or without one's instrument) or even singing. After reviewing notes and rhythm, a logical next step is to review the fingering without playing. (This also applies to other ways a player changes between notes, including trombonists moving their slides and percussionists playing silently in the air above their instruments.)

5. **PERFORM**—Put it all together! Play the music on your instrument normally. Use a slower tempo if necessary. If you do make any mistakes, consider which of the above techniques might help you correct the error.

Look for Musical Patterns

Most music employs patterns in its design, involving some form of repetition. When you spot a rhythm and/or pitch pattern at work in a passage of music, the music becomes easier to play—even predictable! When encountering music for the first time, examine it carefully to see if there might be some pattern to help you grasp the notes and rhythms.

For instance, scan the music to "Aura Lee" below. Can you can spot any patterns at work in the design of this classic folk song?

In fact, many patterns can be found in "Aura Lee," helping to create its pleasing melodic and formal structure. The following example highlights *some* of these. Maybe you've discovered even more!

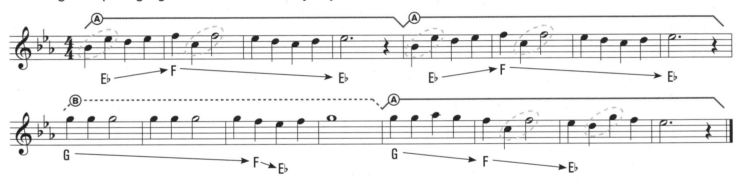

Other ways to help you grasp what's happening in a piece of music will be presented and demonstrated throughout this book, including:

▶ **Recurrence**—literal or near repetition of musical material

▶ **Sequence**—restating a melodic gesture at a different pitch level

▶ **Imitation**—echoing musical material in another's part

▶ **Rule of 3s**—after two statements of a musical idea, the third is often different in some way

Look It Up! (Glossary of Musical Terms)

A glossary of musical terms is included at the end of this book. It should be used to help understand some of the unfamiliar (often foreign language) terms employed by composers to give direction to performers. For instance, each tempo marking listed provides a metronome range (e.g., "*Allegro*, 120–144 beats per minute") and a description of its character (e.g., "Fast, bright"), so you'll know the speed and mood of the music.

When you encounter a musical term or direction that you don't know, *look it up!*

Level 1

WHAT IS A KEY SIGNATURE? Immediately after the clef, composers list which notes are altered by flats or sharps (if any). The flats or sharps are placed on the line(s) or space(s) corresponding to those notes. A key signature remains in effect for the entire piece or until a new key signature is introduced.

KEY OF C MAJOR (CONCERT B♭)

Do you see any flats or sharps in this key signature? If so, how many? Which ones?

KEY OF C MAJOR (Concert B♭)

| 5 | 6 | 7 | 1 | 2 | 3 | 4 | 5 | 6 | 7 | 1 (8) | 2 (9) | 3 (10) | 4 (11) |
| sol | la | ti | do | re | mi | fa | sol | la | ti | do | re | mi | fa |

SCALE is Italian for "ladder" or "stairs." Imagine each note is a step for musicians to climb up and down, beginning and ending on any note. A fun and effective way to gain confidence in a key is to practice ascending and descending notes in various patterns: phone number, birthday, zip code, address, or locker combination for instance. Any series can be used for this challenge. Here are some suggested patterns to get you started:

1 2 3 4 5 4 3 2 1   1 2 1 3 1 4 1 5 1   1 7 1 2 3 1 2 7 1   5 6 7 8 7 6 5 4 5   3 4 5 3 4 2 3 1 2

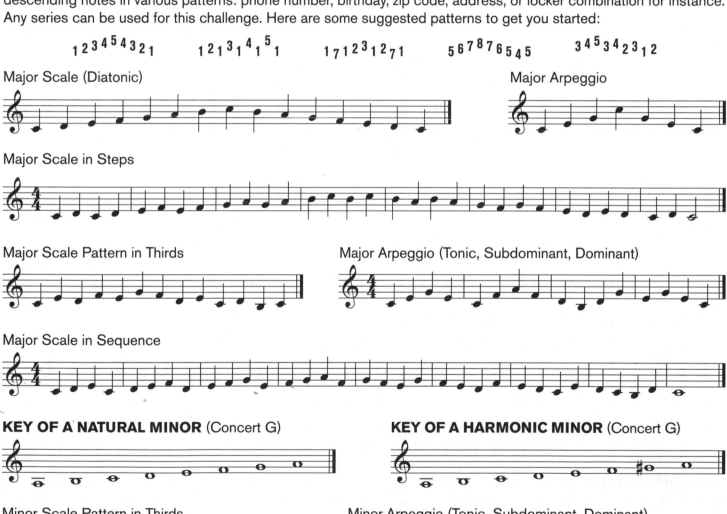

Major Scale (Diatonic)

Major Arpeggio

Major Scale in Steps

Major Scale Pattern in Thirds

Major Arpeggio (Tonic, Subdominant, Dominant)

Major Scale in Sequence

KEY OF A NATURAL MINOR (Concert G)

KEY OF A HARMONIC MINOR (Concert G)

Minor Scale Pattern in Thirds

Minor Arpeggio (Tonic, Subdominant, Dominant)

Minor Scale in Sequence

▶ **Performance Challenge:** Try playing these patterns forward and backward, at faster speeds, and with varied articulations.

TEMPO is the speed at which a piece is performed. Markings, usually in Italian, have a corresponding number that indicate beats per minute (BPM). For example: ♩ = 100 means the piece will be performed at 100 beats per minute.

Largo		Adagio		Andante		Moderato		Allegro		Vivace		Presto	
VERY SLOW			SLOW		MEDIUM			FAST			VERY FAST		
40	54	63	72	80	92	100	116	120	132	144	152	168	176

QUARTER NOTES AND WHOLE NOTES—*Do any of these **measures** contain similar rhythms?*

HIGH OR LOW?—*Do any of the rhythms in this line repeat? How are the rhythms in the first and last measures related?*

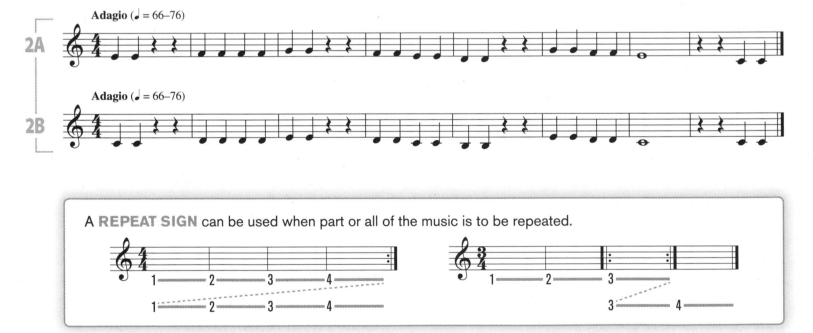

A **REPEAT SIGN** can be used when part or all of the music is to be repeated.

MELODIC CONVERSATION—*Although each of the parts (A and B) rest for a time, the parts form a single **melodic line** when combined. In that way, the parts "complement" each other. Count carefully during the rests!*

DYNAMICS are the markings below the staff that indicate the volume of the music. Dynamic levels remain in effect until a new dynamic marking appears.

pianissimo	*piano*	*mezzo piano*	*mezzo forte*	*forte*	*fortissimo*
very soft	soft	medium soft	medium loud	loud	very loud
pp	*p*	*mp*	*mf*	*f*	*ff*

WATCH YOUR STEP!—*Which measures contain the same rhythms? Be careful when a rhythmic pattern changes! In what way do the **dynamics** follow a pattern? What is the purpose of a **repeat sign**?*

INVERSE CONTOURS—*How do the notes in this example follow a predictable pattern?*

CRESCENDO (*cresc.*) indicates a gradual increase in volume and is represented by this symbol:

DIMINUENDO (*dim.*) or **DECRESCENDO** (*decresc.*) indicates a gradual decrease in volume and is represented by this symbol:

POCO A POCO, Italian for "little by little," can be used when the volume needs to increase or decrease over multiple measures. For example: *cresc. poco a poco* means "increase the volume over several measures."

BUILD, THEN FADE—*Be mindful of the overall dynamic plan of this line. When playing part B, look for any accidentals (flats, sharps, and naturals not in the key signature), so you can anticipate them while playing.*

An **ACCIDENTAL** is a sharp, flat, or natural not in the key signature. It remains in effect for the entire measure.

FADE, THEN BUILD—*Counting rests can sometimes be more challenging than playing notes—count carefully! Lines 6 and 7 have* **complementary rhythms** *and may be performed together. Remember to anticipate accidentals in part B.*

LEAP FROG—*Many of the notes in this example follow a* **pattern**. *Do you see it? The rhythm has more surprises, so count carefully.*

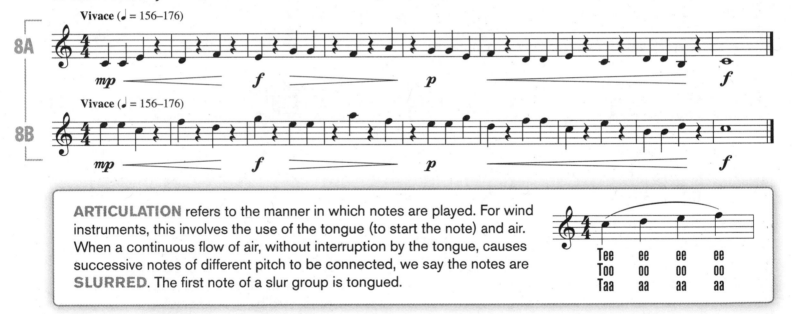

ARTICULATION refers to the manner in which notes are played. For wind instruments, this involves the use of the tongue (to start the note) and air. When a continuous flow of air, without interruption by the tongue, causes successive notes of different pitch to be connected, we say the notes are **SLURRED**. The first note of a slur group is tongued.

Tee	ee	ee	ee
Too	oo	oo	oo
Taa	aa	aa	aa

BACK AND FORTH—*This example features* **slurs** *and a* **melodic sequence**, *a series of notes that form a melodic shape (e.g., measures 1–2 of part A) that moves to different scale degrees. There is* **rhythmic imitation** *between parts A and B. How would you define "rhythmic imitation"?*

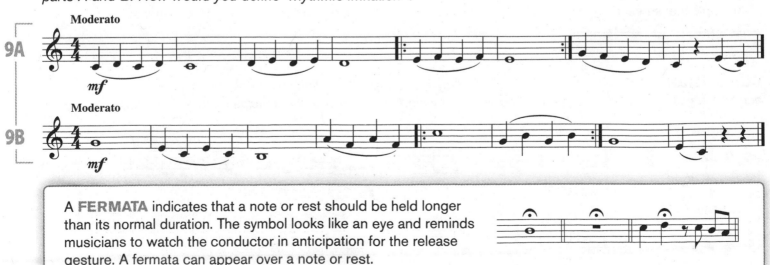

A **FERMATA** indicates that a note or rest should be held longer than its normal duration. The symbol looks like an eye and reminds musicians to watch the conductor in anticipation for the release gesture. A fermata can appear over a note or rest.

9

ECHO CANYON—*The kind of imitation that occurs between parts A and B in this example is known as imitative counterpoint.*

MUSICAL DIALOG—*While there is much use of **rhythmic imitation**, the melodic contour and dynamics vary.*

Music is organized sound and silence with purpose. It is rarely random. When approaching a new piece of music, look carefully and expectantly for **PATTERNS**. Discovering patterns in music reveals more than just the thinking behind its creation. Finding a pattern helps players anticipate what is coming next in the music! Answer these questions:

What is the pattern?　　　How long is it?　　　When does it change?

SURPRISE ENDING—*In what ways is your part predictable? Are there any places where the notes, rhythms, articulations (e.g., slurs), or dynamics seem unexpected?*

PICKUP is a term used when one or more notes lead to the next measure as part of the subsequent phrase.

Quarter notes are commonly used as pickup notes.

Eighth notes are also commonly used as pickup notes.

10

STRENGTH IN NUMBERS—*Count carefully and be sure to bring out the more rhythmically active parts of your line. When a two-beat rest occurs on beats 2 and 3 of a measure (as in measure 8), quarter rests are used.*

SYNOPTIC FANFARE—*Note the use of rhythm (from longer to shorter durations) in this brief, yet exciting example.*

SCHOOL SONG—*Use the dynamics indicated to shape each phrase.*

ROWING LIGHTLY—*This line is comprised of four four-measure phrases. How are they similar? How are they different?*

A FAMILIAR TUNE—*Complementary lines merge to form a familiar melody! Do you recognize this tune?*

MARY *HAD* A LITTLE LAMB!—*We contemplate a sad scenario for Mary and her little lamb with this minor mode version of the familiar tune.*

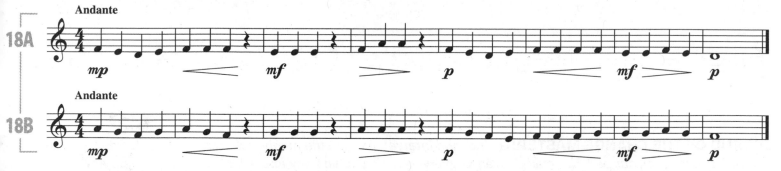

TWINKLE LITTLE STAR—*Another familiar tune, with some **accidentals** in part B, but something seems to be missing! What should be added to complete this piece? (Hint: Think about how repetition is used in this song.)*

A CHANGE OF PART—*This longer passage is more indicative of an actual piece. Listen well to decide if your part sounds like the **melody** or the **accompaniment**...and watch out for accidentals!*

A CHANGE OF PART (ROLE REVERSAL)—*Here, as is often the case in music, a player's part experiences a "role reversal" as it shifts between **melody** and **accompaniment**, and vice versa.*

12

READY FOR CHANGE—*Another piece in which your role shifts between* **melody** *and* **accompaniment**.

READY FOR CHANGE (ROLE REVERSAL)

LEGEND OF THE CHANGE MASTERS—*The term* **interval** *refers to the number of scale steps between two notes. Examine your part for small and larger intervals. Can you find any intervallic patterns? Is there any correlation between the dynamics and the size of the intervals?*

LEGEND OF THE CHANGE MASTERS (ROLE REVERSAL)

TIMBRE is tone color and refers both to a specific instrument's sound as well as the combined sound of groups of instruments. As one section softens while another gets louder, a change in color is heard rather than a change in volume!

SHIFTING COLORS—*This is an example of how dynamics can turn one **tonal color** into another. Here, n is used as a dynamic abbreviation for **niente**, which means to fade into nothing. Reminder: **Accidentals** stay in effect during **all notes of a tie**.*

SHIFTING COLORS (ROLE REVERSAL)—*Allow your sound to grow out of the previous color and fade into the next.*

Rhythm Grid 1

A rhythm grid functions as a glossary of rhythms covered in each level. This can serve as a check point to determine if a musician is ready to advance to the next unit. The measures in each grid can be read in any direction and begin or end at any point, offering exponential combinations of rhythms. This grid covers $\frac{4}{4}$ rhythms used in Level 1.

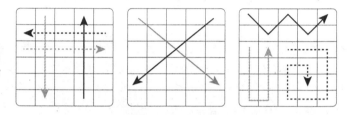

Level 2

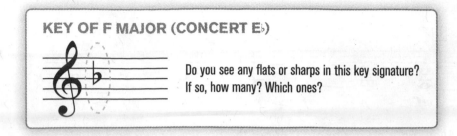

KEY OF F MAJOR (CONCERT E♭)

Do you see any flats or sharps in this key signature?
If so, how many? Which ones?

KEY OF F MAJOR (Concert E♭)

| 5 | 6 | 7 | 1 | 2 | 3 | 4 | 5 | 6 | 7 | 1 (8) | 2 (9) | 3 (10) | 4 (11) |
| sol | la | ti | do | re | mi | fa | sol | la | ti | do | re | mi | fa |

Major Scale (Diatonic)

Major Arpeggio

Major Scale in Steps

Major Scale Pattern in Thirds

Major Arpeggio (Tonic, Subdominant, Dominant)

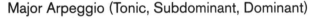

Major Scale in Sequence

KEY OF D NATURAL MINOR (Concert C)

KEY OF D HARMONIC MINOR (Concert C)

Minor Scale Pattern in Thirds

Minor Arpeggio (Tonic, Subdominant, Dominant)

Minor Scale in Sequence

DYNAMIC CHORALE—*Dynamics* remain in effect until something new is indicated. What is the dynamic level at measure 4? How about at measure 6?

PATTERN SEARCH—*How are measures 1–2 related to measures 3–4? Is there a pattern? How about measures 5–6?*

RITE OF PASSAGE—*What is the **melodic pattern** used in part A? Practice performing this line at **various tempi**. Listen to others as you play your part, working to maintain **balance** as the harmony becomes more complex.*

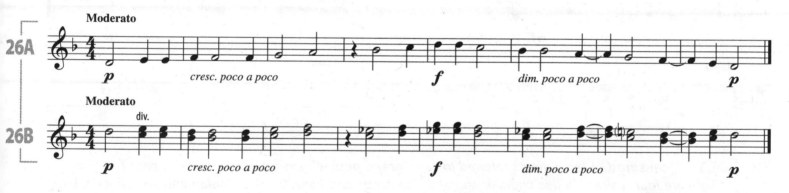

Composers use an **ACCENT** when they want to give a note emphasis. Woodwind and brass musicians accent notes by using more air at the front of the note and with a firmer articulation. Percussionists accent notes by using a higher stick height (and more force) or a harder mallet choice.

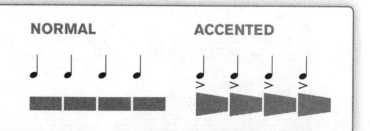

FOCUS ON ACCENTS—*Play **accented notes** with extra emphasis. Play at different dynamic levels to practice performing **accents** at those levels.*

COMPENDIUM—In the following line, put your skill in observing **melodic** and **rhythmic patterns**, **dynamic changes**, and **accents** to the test!

RHYTHM IN DISGUISE—Note the different ways in which a three-beat duration occurs in the music.

THE MOTION WITHIN—Listen for **moving notes** in other parts when playing longer note values.

TIME OUT—A **caesura** (///) (sometimes referred to as a **"grand pause"**) indicates a brief, silent pause in the music. There are four "voices" in this chorale: soprano, alto, tenor, and bass. Work on **balancing** your voice part with the others.

FINLANDIA—When **changing keys**, scan your part for notes affected by the new **key signature**.

Jean Sibelius

TRIBUTE—*Compare measures 1–4 with 5–8. What is the same? What is different?*

EPIC JOURNEY—*The **melodic** and **dynamic** arc to and from the **climax** in measure 6 creates musical drama.*

TROIS UN—*What is the **dynamic level** following the **repeated section**? Can you find a **rhythmic pattern** employed in the music?*

WHOLE LOT OF RESTS—***Whole rests** last for the entire measure, regardless of the time signature. Count carefully because parts A and B together form a unison melody. Practice at various tempi.*

WINTER WALTZ—*Can you discern the three components of the music: **melody**, **accompaniment**, and **bass line**? Practice performing all three parts.*

TOGETHER AS ONE—*As you perform this flowing chorale, listen for* **moving quarter notes** *in other parts while playing longer note values, and observe the* **time signature change** *in measure 5.*

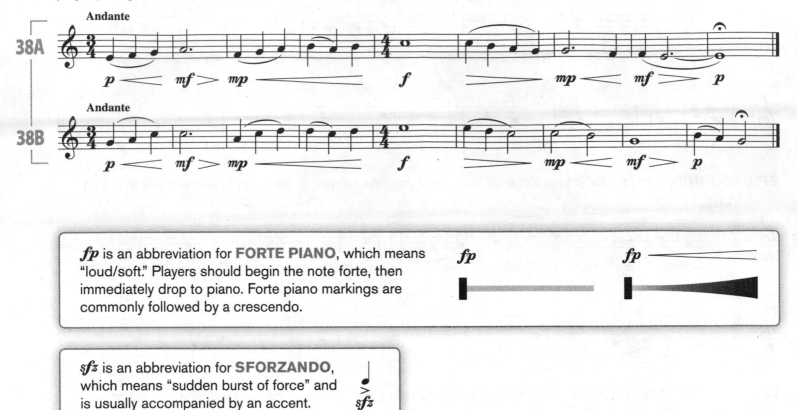

fp is an abbreviation for **FORTE PIANO**, which means "loud/soft." Players should begin the note forte, then immediately drop to piano. Forte piano markings are commonly followed by a crescendo.

sfz is an abbreviation for **SFORZANDO**, which means "sudden burst of force" and is usually accompanied by an accent.

STURM UND DRANG—*Forte piano* (*fp*) *indicates a strong, loud attack followed immediately by a soft dynamic level. The effect is dramatic! This line demonstrates several ways a composer might indicate* **releasing a held note** *on beat 1 of the following measure.*

DYNAMIC DRAMA—*Sforzando* (*sfz*) *indicates a sudden, loud accent. Be careful to observe the* **changes in meter** *throughout.*

19

UNDER THE BIG TOP—*Practice performing all three components of the music: the **melody**, **accompaniment**, and **bass line**.*

DANZA DEI SETTE—*Briefly, but carefully, examine this example that employs measures of **alternating meter**. Then close your book and list as many of the **expressive markings** as you can. How observant were you?*

EXCERPT FROM SYMPHONY NO. 2—*Listen for **moving half** and **quarter notes** in other parts while playing longer whole and half notes.*

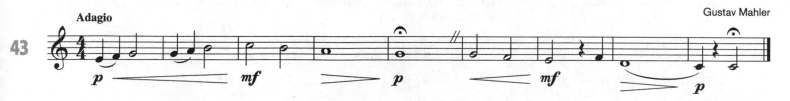

EXCERPT FROM SYMPHONY NO. 2—*Here's the same music in a **different key**, and you may have a different part as well. What is a benefit of being able to perform a piece in different keys?*

20

COMING HOME—*Where are the most challenging parts of this music? What strategies can help you play them correctly on your first try?*

SONG OF THE SERAPHIM—*Accidentals are used throughout to create captivating harmonies in this piece.*

SONG OF THE SERAPHIM (ROLE REVERSAL)—*What are some musical concerns to consider when your part takes on a different role?*

Rhythm Grid 2.1

This grid covers rhythms used in Level 2, plus other rhythms commonly associated with these note values as they appear in $\frac{4}{4}$ **time**. Ask your director how the tied notes are to be performed.

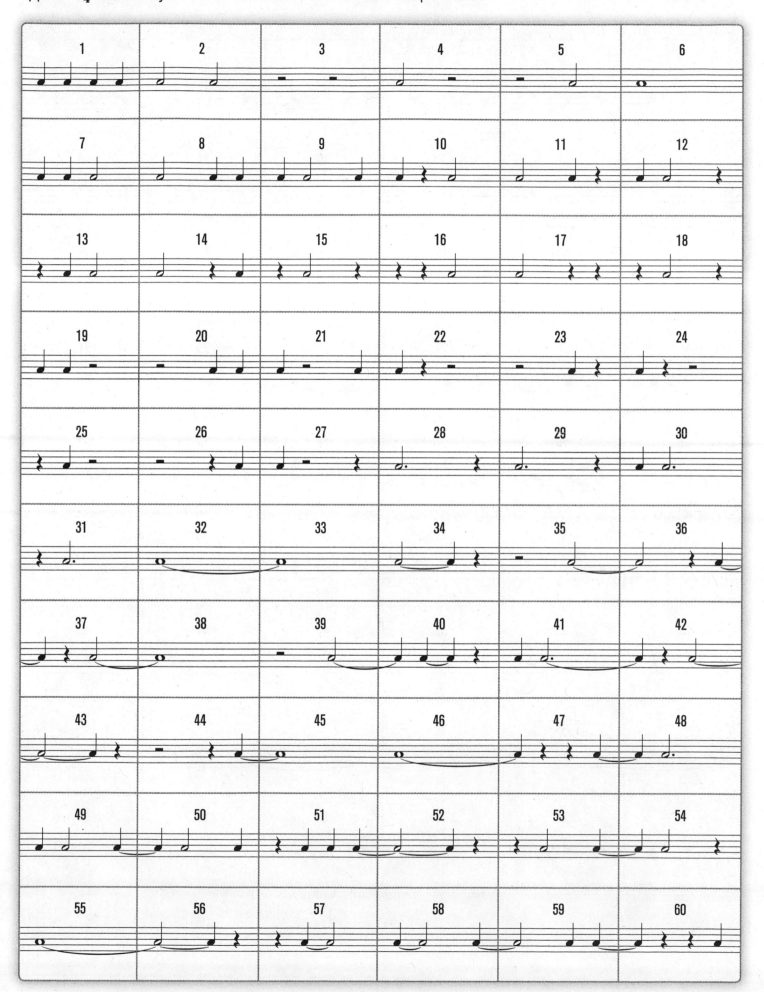

Rhythm Grid 2.2

This grid covers additional rhythms used in Level 2, plus other rhythms commonly associated with these note values as they appear in ¾ **time**. Ask your director how the tied notes are to be performed.

Level 3

KEY OF G MAJOR (CONCERT F)

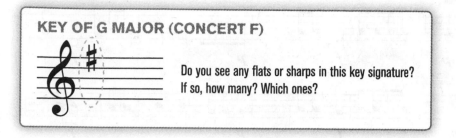

Do you see any flats or sharps in this key signature?
If so, how many? Which ones?

KEY OF G MAJOR (Concert F)

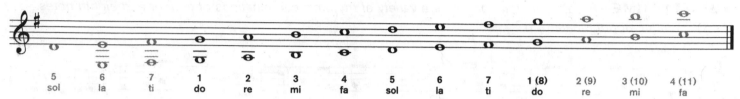

5	6	7	1	2	3	4	5	6	7	1 (8)	2 (9)	3 (10)	4 (11)
sol	la	ti	do	re	mi	fa	sol	la	ti	do	re	mi	fa

Major Scale (Diatonic)

Major Arpeggio

Major Scale in Steps

Major Scale Pattern in Thirds

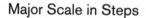

Major Arpeggio (Tonic, Subdominant, Dominant)

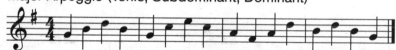
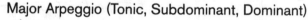

Major Scale in Sequence

KEY OF E NATURAL MINOR (Concert D)

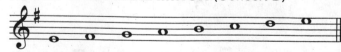

KEY OF E HARMONIC MINOR (Concert D)

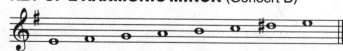

Minor Scale Pattern in Thirds

Minor Arpeggio (Tonic, Subdominant, Dominant)

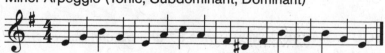
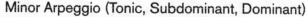

Minor Scale in Sequence

STEPS TO THE THRONE—This line employs several immediate (or "terraced") dynamic shifts. Do the changing quarter and eighth notes in this line follow any pattern?

A SHIFT IN TIME—Be alert as you encounter a variety of rhythmic combinations of quarter and eighth notes. What is unique about measure 6?

SOLEMN VOX—There is rhythmic independence between parts A and B, so count carefully!

TOP SECRET—Your mission, should you choose to accept it, is to decipher the following musical codes: part A–**44212341** and part B–**32431412**. What do they mean?

YOU COMPLETE ME—Lines 51 and 52 can be performed together. They "complement" each other. Count carefully during the rests!

YOU COMPLETE ME, TOO—*Lines 51 and 52 can be performed together. They "complement" each other. Count carefully during the rests!*

LEGATO is an articulation marking that instructs musicians to connect notes together with a smooth air stream. A legato note will "touch" the next note.

STACCATO is an articulation marking that instructs musicians to put some space between notes. A staccato note will not "touch" the next note.

SHAPE SHIFTER—*Demonstrate your ability to play legato and staccato notes in this line.*

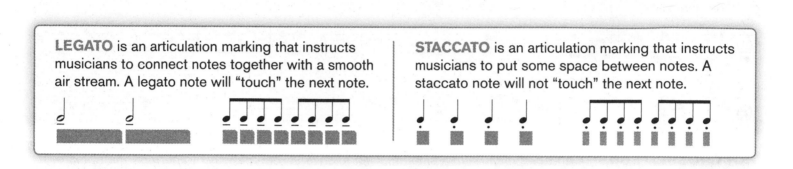

1ST AND 2ND ENDINGS are used to conserve space on the page when much of the music is repeated.

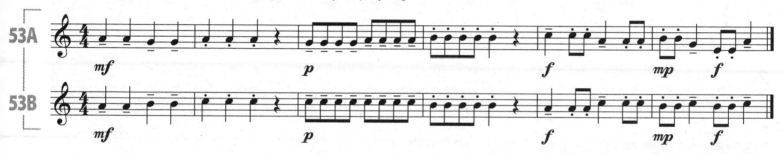

1st time ⟶
2nd time ⟶ Skip over the 1st ending the 2nd time. ⟶

WALKIN' COOL—*What patterns can you find in this happy tune with its infectious groove?*

Scott Watson

BAND HALL ROCK—*This line, in rock style, is an example of 12-bar blues. Before performing, scan your music for the different articulations used (staccato, legato, slur, and accent).*

HOT CROSSED BUNS—*Cantabile means "in a smooth, singing style." What are ways to perform the notes of this familiar children's tune in such a manner?*

> **D.C. AL FINE**—D.C. is an abbreviation for *Da Capo*, meaning "the head" or "from the beginning," and *al Fine* means "to the end." D.C. al Fine means "return to the beginning and continue playing to the Fine."

TWINKLE² LITTLE STAR—*When performed as indicated, how many measures long will it be?*

TWINKLE³ LITTLE STAR—*Here is a lovely, triple meter arrangement of "Twinkle, Twinkle Little Star"!*

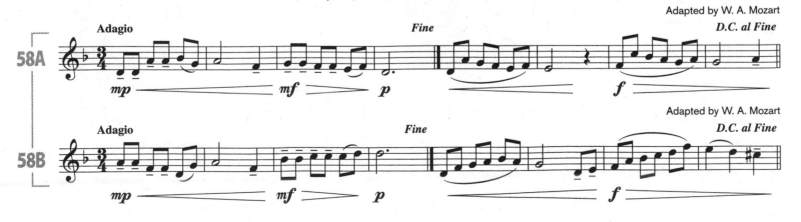

LITTLE BUNNY FOO FOO—*Another familiar folk song, with a twist!*

LITTLE BUNNY FOO FOO, IN MEMORIAM—*A sad requiem for that dear, but mischievous, bunny rabbit.*

DANCE OF THE GOOD KING—*Pay close attention to the various articulation markings and dynamic levels used in this line.*

28

YANKEE DOODLE—*Perform this well-known American song with even tonguing.*

American Traditional

62A

YANKEE DOODLE (STACCATO)—*Perform this staccato version of the tune.*

American Traditional

62B

YANKEE DOODLE (LEGATO)—*Perform this legato version of the tune.*

American Traditional

62C

YANKEE DOODLE (TONGUE 2, SLUR 2)—*Staccatos, slurs, and some legato.*

American Traditional

62D

YANKEE DOODLE (SLUR 2, TONGUE 2)—*Slurs, staccatos, and some legato.*

American Traditional

62E

YANKEE DOODLE (TTST)—*Staccato, two slurred, staccato.*

American Traditional

62F

YANKEE DOODLE (TTTS)—*Staccato with slurs over the bar line.*

American Traditional

62G

ORPHEUS IN THE UNDERWORLD—*This well-known work is often referred to as the "Can-Can."*

Jacques Offenbach

63A Allegro

Jacques Offenbach

63B Allegro

STRESS RAPTURE—*Analyze the notes, rhythms, and accents in this line for patterns. What do you find?*

64

FIESTA DE BAILE—*Fiesta de Baile, or "dance party," uses elements of samba music. Special attention should be paid to articulations.*

FIESTA DE BAILE (ROLE REVERSAL)

READY TO SHINE—*After a brief, somber opening, the music gives way to a bright and joyful mood.*

READY TO SHINE (ROLE REVERSAL)

Rhythm Grid 3.1

This grid covers ¼ rhythms used in Level 3, plus other rhythms commonly associated with duple eighth notes. **Duple eighth notes** are eighth notes that appear in groups of two or four and are usually beamed together.

Rhythm Grid 3.2

This grid covers additional $\frac{4}{4}$ rhythms used in Level 3, plus other rhythms commonly associated with duple eighth notes and **ties**. Ask your director how the tied notes are to be performed.

Level 4

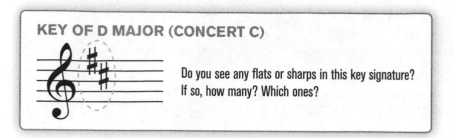

KEY OF D MAJOR (Concert C)

5	6	7	1	2	3	4	5	6	7	1 (8)	2 (9)	3 (10)	4 (11)
sol	la	ti	do	re	mi	fa	sol	la	ti	do	re	mi	fa

Major Scale (Diatonic)

Major Arpeggio

Major Scale in Steps

Major Scale Pattern in Thirds

Major Arpeggio (Tonic, Subdominant, Dominant)

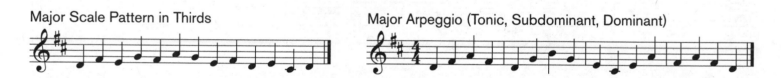

Major Scale in Sequence

KEY OF B NATURAL MINOR (Concert A)

KEY OF B HARMONIC MINOR (Concert A)

Minor Scale Pattern in Thirds

Minor Arpeggio (Tonic, Subdominant, Dominant)

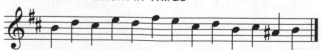

Minor Scale in Sequence

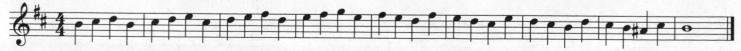

34

INTRADA—*Eighth notes* may appear in music beamed together or separate (single). Do you know what usually determines this? Play this line first *Adagio* with *legato* tonguing, then *Allegro* with *staccato* tonguing.

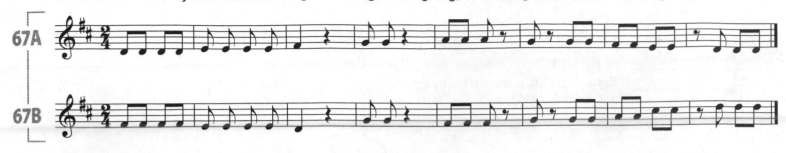

DOWNBEAT is used to refer to the start of a beat, the moment when a player's foot touches the floor while tapping. **UPBEAT** refers to the point exactly halfway between downbeats, when the player's foot is in the air.

SKINNY BUNNY FOO FOO—*Many eighth notes in this line are beamed together. Why are some eighth notes separate, with "flags"? Play this line first Andante with legato tonguing, then Allegro with staccato tonguing.*

CRAZY EIGHTHS—*Twice in measure 6 we find the use of two consecutive eighth rests. What is the advantage of using a pair of eighth rest in these locations instead of quarter rests? Play this line first Moderato with legato tonguing, then Allegro with staccato tonguing.*

EXPANDING POSSIBILITIES—*Note the many eighth-note/eighth-rest patterns throughout this line. What do measures 1–4 all have in common? How is measure 5 related to measure 6? Play this line first Adagio with legato tonguing, then Allegro with staccato tonguing.*

HOCKET—*Hocket is the medieval practice of dividing the notes of a melody between two parts. Practice each part (A and B) separately, then perform them together to hear the hocket!*

ISOLATED EIGHTHS—*In this "**retrograde duet**," one group plays normally as another group performs the part backwards. Try it…but count carefully for it to work!*

SUBDIVIDE AND CONQUER—*Subdividing means to think and count the smallest rhythmic unit in the music while playing. Counting subdivisions keeps the steady quarter-note beat of part B from accelerating. Counting subdivisions helps part A perform eighth notes/rests with accurate timing.*

AGENT ACCENT UNDER ARREST!—*You must crack the code, **34212413**, in order to free Agent Accent from enemy hands! What does it mean?*

VANISHING EIGHTHS—*Scan for the beat location of eighth rests before performing this line.*

DECK THE HALLS WITH RANDOM EIGHTH NOTES—*The appearance of unexpected eighth notes and rests throughout this line make it both challenging and fun!*

Welsh Carol

G__D KIN_ WEN_E_LAS—*Here's an example of complementary rhythms in parts A and B working together to create one complete melody, the familiar holiday tune "Good King Wenceslas."*

13th-century Finnish Carol

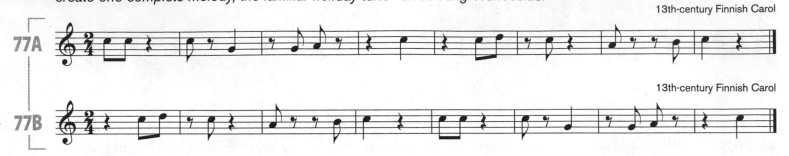

KIT AND KABOODLE—*Why are some eighth notes beamed together in pairs, while others are not?*

SHAFTS OF LIGHT—*Hold note durations for their full value, especially leading up to rests.*

AT HALF PAST ONE—*Compare the rhythm in measures 1, 3, and 5. How are they related?*

CANTEC TRIST—*Compare the stepwise melodic motion of part A with the up-and-down interval leaps in part B.*

MY RAGTIME GAL—*Ragtime, an early jazz-style music featuring lively syncopations often in a quick-paced tempo, enjoyed its peak around the turn of the 20th-century.*

Joseph Howard and Ida Emerson

Joseph Howard and Ida Emerson

RISE TO THE OCCASION—*A slow, lush introduction is followed by a faster, optimistic main theme. What role does articulation play in defining the sound of these contrasting sections?*

HERCULES VS. THE HYDRA—*As you play, listen and respond to the exciting interaction between parts A and B. At times a double bar is used to indicate a new section of music.*

Scott Watson

ARABIAN DANCE (LE CAFÉ)—*"Arabian Dance" comes from Peter Ilyich Tchaikovsky's most famous ballet,* The Nutcracker. *What part of the world does the music suggest to you?*

P. I. Tchaikovsky

ARABIAN DANCE (LE CAFÉ)—*This version of "Arabian Dance" allows you to explore a different part of the arrangement. Would you describe the part you played in 85A as melody, accompaniment, or bass line? How would you describe the part you play in 85B?*

P. I. Tchaikovsky

Rhythm Grid 4.1

This grid covers 4/4 rhythms used in Level 4, plus other rhythms commonly associated with single eighth notes.
Single eighth notes are eighth notes that appear by themselves and are not beamed together. Instead, they have a flag attached to the stem.

Rhythm Grid 4.2

This grid covers additional $\frac{4}{4}$ rhythms used in Level 4, plus other rhythms commonly associated with duple and single eighth notes.

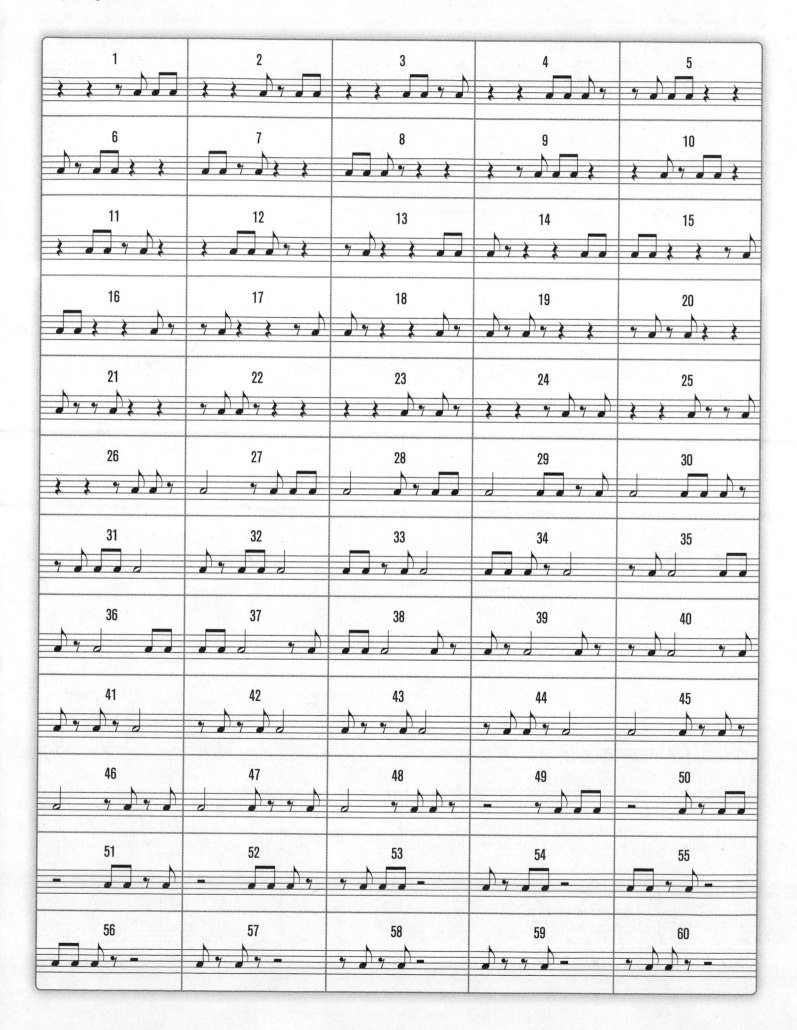

Rhythm Grid 4.3

This grid covers even more $\frac{4}{4}$ rhythms used in Level 4, plus other rhythms commonly associated with eighth notes, ties, and syncopation. **SYNCOPATION** is when a rhythm emphasizes the upbeat (the weaker part of the beat).

Level 5

KEY OF B♭ MAJOR (CONCERT A♭)

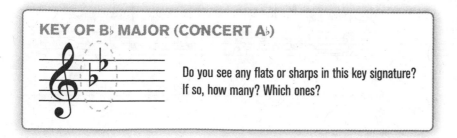

Do you see any flats or sharps in this key signature?
If so, how many? Which ones?

KEY OF B♭ MAJOR (Concert A♭)

5	6	7	1 (8)	2	3	4	5	6	7	1 (8)	2 (9)	3 (10)	4 (11)
sol	la	ti	do	re	mi	fa	sol	la	ti	do	re	mi	fa

Major Scale (Diatonic)

Major Arpeggio

Major Scale in Steps

Major Scale Pattern in Thirds

Major Arpeggio (Tonic, Subdominant, Dominant)

Major Scale in Sequence

KEY OF G NATURAL MINOR (Concert F)

KEY OF G HARMONIC MINOR (Concert F)

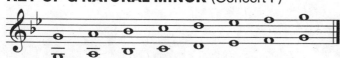

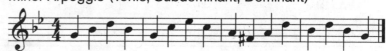

Minor Scale Pattern in Thirds

Minor Arpeggio (Tonic, Subdominant, Dominant)

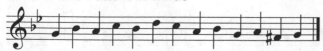

Minor Scale in Sequence

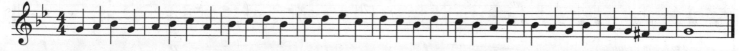

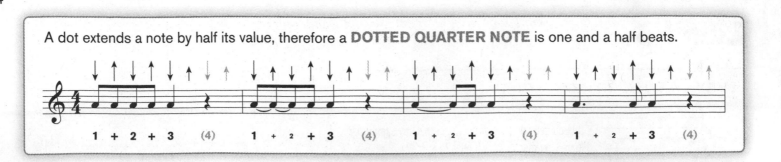

A dot extends a note by half its value, therefore a **DOTTED QUARTER NOTE** is one and a half beats.

THREE IN ONE—*Note how **three eighth notes** fit in the space of a **dotted quarter note**.*

AMERICA, THE BEAUTIFUL—*This beautiful song has been arranged in **four parts**: **part A** is the **melody**, **part B** is one of the **harmony** parts. Find some friends to perform it with all four parts, taking turns playing the melody.*

Samuel A. Ward

IN RARA DUO—*The dotted-quarter-note rhythm appears several times throughout this line, always on beat 1, 2, or 3 of the measure, but never beat 4. Why?*

45

HOLD ON—*Be sure to hold each dotted quarter note for its full value before moving to the note that follows.*

SILENT NIGHT—*In this arrangement, the notes of the familiar tune are passed from instrument to instrument. Bring out the melody when you have it.*

Franz Gruber

DÉJÀ VU—*Part A is based on a melody from Level 4. Can you guess which one?*

GRAIL QUEST—*This line features the dotted quarter note followed by multiple eighth notes.*

LARGO FROM SYMPHONY NO. 9, "FROM THE NEW WORLD"—*Czech composer Antonín Dvořák wrote Symphony No. 9 in 1893 while living in the United States. It is based on African-American spirituals and Native-American folk music.*

ANGELS WE HAVE HEARD ON HIGH—*The music for this well-known carol comes from an old French song.*

SLAVIC THEME—*This song has been arranged in **four parts**: **part A** is the **melody**, and **part B** is one of the* ***harmony*** *parts. Find some friends to perform it with all four parts, taking turns playing the melody.*

SUO GÁN—*This line contains five **fermatas** and several **meter changes**. Watch your director carefully!*

48

EINE KLEINE NOTE MUSIK—*When the dotted-quarter/eighth-note rhythm is followed by a rest, the eighth note should be played* **staccato** *so it "pops." Just like little brothers and sisters, this "little note" needs lots of attention!*

MARY'S LAMB LEAPING ON AND OFF THE BEAT—*It might be helpful to write the counts for this tricky line before playing it. Be sure to observe the many "style markings"* (**articulations**) *throughout!*

SOMEWHERE, OVER THE BAR LINE—*Although it would be impossible to have a dotted quarter note on beat 4, a* **quarter note tied over the bar to an eighth note** *accomplishes the same thing.*

IT TAKES A VILLAGE (PEOPLE)—*Syncopation* (unexpected rhythmic stress, usually on upbeats), comes in *several forms in this line.*

JAMAICA ME CRAZY—*Characteristic Caribbean syncopations drive this island treat!*

Scott Watson

JAMAICA ME CRAZY (ROLE REVERSAL)—*Same fun, new role.*

Scott Watson

Rhythm Grid 5

This grid covers $\frac{4}{4}$ rhythms used in Level 5, plus other rhythms commonly associated with a **dotted quarter note**/ eighth note and ties.

Level 6

GRAND PROCESSION—Bring out the **moving notes** in your part. When playing with others, **listen** for their moving notes.

CHANGE OF TIME—In $\frac{6}{4}$ time, the quarter note gets the beat. In $\frac{6}{8}$ time, the eighth note gets the beat. For this reason, the $\frac{6}{4}$ example sounds identical to the $\frac{6}{8}$ example!

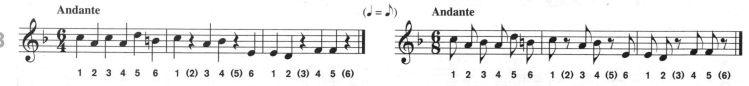

BEAM ME UP!—In $\frac{6}{8}$ time, it is common to beam together the first three eighth notes and the last three eighth notes of each measure.

MERRY BAND OF FRIENDS—Tapping your foot with the eighth note at 216 BPM is difficult! Therefore, in this case, musicians would normally tap a **dotted-quarter pulse** of 72 BPM instead.

VICTOR'S SONG—How many beats does a dotted quarter note receive?

52

MARY'S DANCING LAMB—*The notation of measures 1–4 and 5–8 are both common ways to illustrate a **lifted style** of playing in* §*time. Although they look different on the staff, the style should sound the same.*

MIDNIGHT AT THE CIRCUS—*Practice counting and performing this line **without the ties** first, then (when confident and comfortable with the rhythm) perform as is, with the ties.*

WHEN JOHNNY COMES MARCHING HOME—*This folk song in* § *time was popularized during the American Civil War and expressed people's longing for soldiers to return home. The melody employs **pickup notes** in several locations.*

American Folk Song

American Folk Song

MOVEMENT 3 FROM *A LONGFORD LEGEND*—*The* § *time signature contributes to the delightful, Celtic sound of this music, inspired by Irish street ballads.*

Robert Sheldon

Robert Sheldon

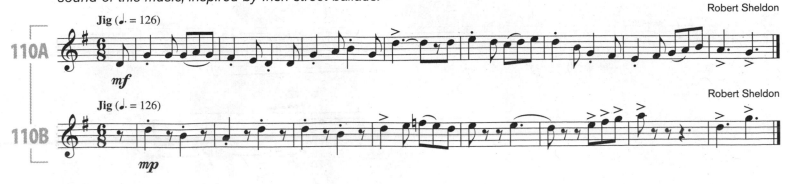

DOWN THE BOULEVARD (MARCH)—*This line, like so many marches, is set in a brisk* $\frac{6}{8}$ *meter with a* **dotted-quarter-note pulse.**

CANCIÓN DE OTOÑO—*This hauntingly beautiful song requires graceful execution. Before performing, observe the changes of key, review fingerings for accidentals in your part, and think through the varied* $\frac{6}{8}$ *rhythms used.*

> **ENHARMONIC** is a term for when the same pitch has two different names. Like homophones, enharmonics sound the same but have different spelling and harmonic functions.

ALSO KNOWN AS (A.K.A.)—*The term enharmonic refers to a different spelling (or alias) for a note. Every note has an enharmonic equivalent. For instance, F♯ is also known as G♭. D♯ is also known as E♭. Can you name some others?*

113A

113B

TWOS AND THREES—*Just as the number six is divisible by two and three, the* **pulse in ⁶⁄₈** *time can be felt in* **two or three.** *Accents in this line highlight whether measures should be felt in two or in three.*

114A Allegro

114B Allegro

FROM "PALACIO REAL"—*The music of this line alternates rhythmic pulse from two to three.*

Brian Beck

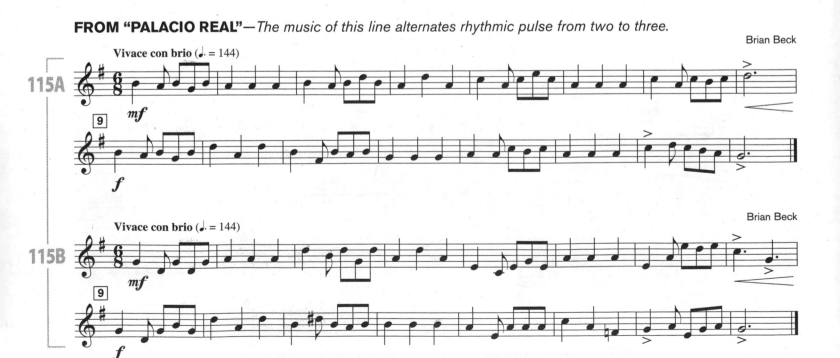

115A Vivace con brio (♩. = 144)

115B Vivace con brio (♩. = 144)

Brian Beck

D.S. AL FINE—D.S. is an abbreviation for *Dal Segno*, meaning "the sign," and *al Fine* means "to the end." D.S. al Fine means "return to the sign 𝄋 and continue playing to the Fine."

JARABE TAPATÍO—*Before performing this beloved Mexican folk song, known to some as the "Mexican Hat Dance," be sure to review challenging rhythms, accidentals, and the formal "roadmap" (e.g., **D.S. al Fine**).*

Traditional Mexican Folk Dance

Rhythm Grid 6

This grid covers rhythms used in Level 6, plus other rhythms commonly associated with dotted quarter note/eighth note and ties in $\frac{6}{8}$ **time**.

Articulation and Style Grid

This grid covers 4/4 rhythms with various articulations and styles covered in this book. Please remember to read ahead and anticipate any upcoming changes.

Glossary of Musical Terms

a tempo – Return to the original tempo.

accent (>) – Play the note with a strong attack.

accidentals (♯♭♮) – Sharps, flats, and naturals aside from those in the key signature.

Adagietto – Fairly slow.

Adagio – A slow tempo.

Agitato – Play in an agitated manner.

Alla marcia – In the style of a march.

Allegro – A fast tempo.

Andante – A moderate walking tempo.

caesura (//) – A brief period of silence.

cantabile – In a smooth, singing style.

crescendo (———) – Gradually play louder.

D.C. (Da Capo) al Fine – Repeat from the beginning and play to the Fine.

D.S. (Dal Segno) al Fine – Repeat from the 𝄋 and play to the Fine.

decrescendo or **diminuendo** (———) – Gradually play softer.

duet – A composition for two performers.

dynamics – Change in volume.

enharmonic – Refers to two notes that sound the same but have different names (F♯ and G♭).

espressivo – Play with feeling.

fermata (𝄐) – To hold a note or rest longer than its normal duration.

flat (♭) – Lowers the pitch of a note a half step.

forte piano (fp) – Play loudly, then immediately softly.

forte-piano (f–p) – Play loudly the first time, then softly on the repeat.

forte (f) – Play loudly.

fortissimo (ff) – Play very loudly.

grand pause – A long period of silence in the music.

jig – A lively Irish dance, usually in $\frac{6}{8}$ time.

Largo – A slow tempo.

legato – An articulation or style of playing that is smooth and connected.

marcato (ᴧ) – Played with emphasis; accented.

mezzo forte (mf) – Medium loud.

mezzo piano (mp) – Medium soft.

Misterioso – Played in a mysterious mood.

Moderato – A medium tempo.

molto – Very, great.

natural (♮) – Cancels out a sharp or flat.

niente (n) – Fade to nothing.

non troppo – Not too much.

ostinato – A repeated phrase or rhythm.

pesante – Heavy, full of sound.

piano (p) – Play softly.

piano (pp) – Play very softly.

poco a poco – Little by little.

ragtime – A musical style pre-dating jazz that uses syncopation.

rallentando (*rall.*) – Gradually becoming slower.

ritardando (*rit.*) – Gradually becoming slower.

sforzando (sf) – A sudden or strong accent.

sharp (♯) – Raises the pitch of a note a half step.

slur – A curved line connecting two or more notes of different pitches; tongue only the first note in a slur.

staccato (·) – An articulation or style of playing that is light and separated.

subito – Immediately, suddenly.

tempo – The speed of the music.

tie – A curved line connecting two or more notes of the same pitch; tongue only the first note.

Vivace – Lively, quick.

Vivo – Lively and spirited.

Clarinet Fingering Chart

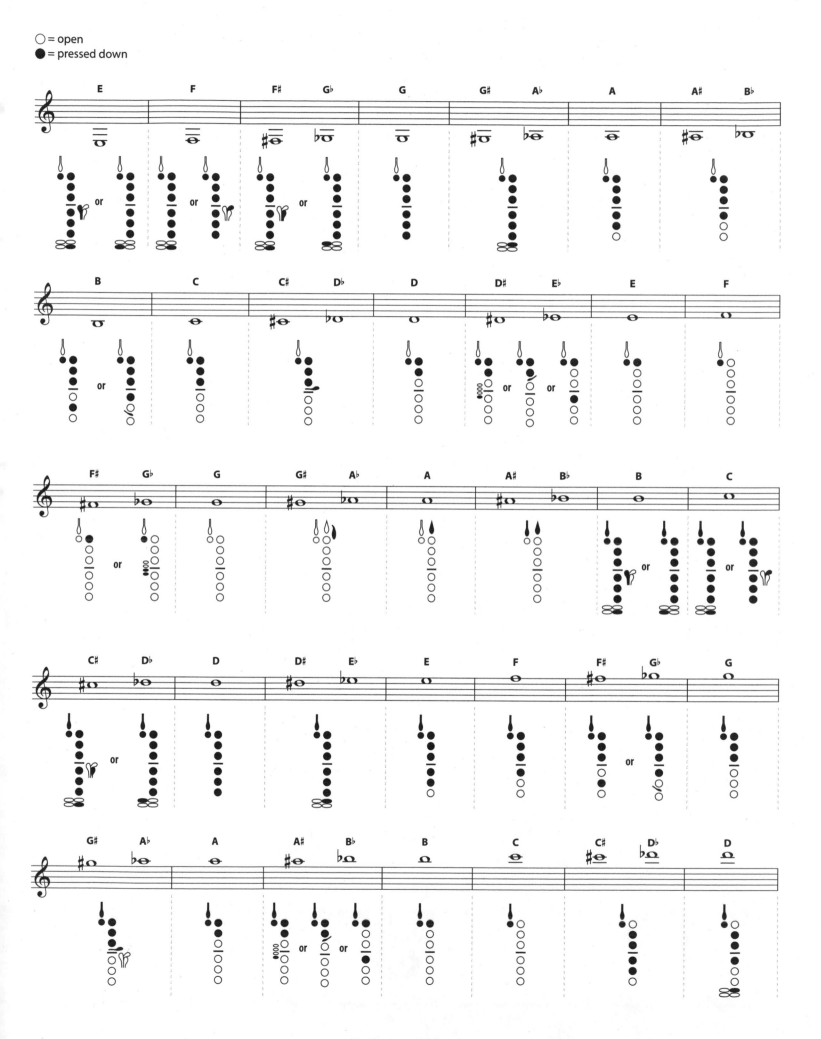